Got challenges?

Depression is…..depressing.
Stress is…..stressful.
Grief, loss, anxiety,
physical and mental health issues,
addiction, family issues, and more,
- life itself.
All are challenging.
All can be managed.

When you don't know if you can even get out of bed, a big book full of little words can be overwhelming. Here are **101 Tools to Build a Good Life.** These tools came from my own education and experiences, both professional and personal.

These are short and practical "tools" you can sort through, choose, and use right away, then add to your

personal toolkit to **Build a Good Life.**

101 Tools to
Build A Good Life

Manage Life's Challenges

Laurie Kimball RN, M.S.
AGoodLife4U.com

Dedication:

To YOU!
And to ME!
To all of us who have faced
our challenges
over and over and over
and over again.
We keep getting up and trying again.
Life *is* a challenge.
We learn to plan and practice
to manage all our challenges.

Thank you to those who live with us
and those who help us get up again.

Please use these tools to
Build a Good Life for yourself!

101 Tools to Build a Good Life

Manage Life's Challenges

Contents:

Begin Building

A Good Life For You

Consider these three questions:
What does a good life mean to me?
What are challenges in my good life?
What tools help me build a good life?

If you know me, I have asked you these questions. If you don't know me, I would like to ask you also. Well? I know what a good life is - for me. Is it the same for everyone? When we watch TV, we see countless commercials. We see advertisements in magazines and newspapers, on billboards, buses, and cars. We hear them on the radio. Advertising has one purpose — to make you dissatisfied. Dissatisfied with yourself, your possessions, your life. "If you buy our product, you will be happy!" But that's not true, is it?

Laurie Kimball

Don't let others tell you what you want or need. Make time to figure out for yourself what your good life is, what your challenges are, and what tools help you to build that good life.

As a result of asking people these three questions, I have noted that material possessions rarely make the list for a good life.

Over and over it was faith, family, friends, love, happiness, health, peace, freedom, meaningful work, support, energy, satisfaction, helping others, and education on people's lists. Fishing and pets made it, too! The only mention of money as part of a good life has been financial stability.

There are obstacles, or challenges, to every good life. There are also tools to help you manage these challenges so you can *Build a Good Life*. That is what this book is all about.

What would a
psych nurse say?

This book came from my 40 years as a Registered Nurse, 20 years as an inpatient psychiatric nurse, and several years as a therapist. Before and during these professional experiences, I had many difficult winters, not quite knowing why my life seemed so much harder than it used to be. When spring came, I put that challenge behind me, thinking I was fine. Then winter came again! Year after year, the same hard season returned, until I was diagnosed with Seasonal Affective Disorder and learned how to manage my seasonal depression and other life challenges. My own experiences and those of people I have worked with have all led to writing this book. As a psych nurse, I would ask you to ask yourself some questions during your life's challenges.

Laurie Kimball

- Am I safe? Where am I safe?
- What is going on in my life?
- Am I experiencing this challenge for the first time?
- Have I had a medical checkup?
- What has changed in my life, relationships, hobbies, family, health, work, habits, lifestyle?
- Am I taking good care of myself?

I'm telling you *now* what I wish I had been told *then* during the hardest challenges in my life:

- Don't wait for a crisis
- Manage challenges right away
- Don't go it alone. Get help
- Know my triggers and strengths
- Quit bad habits
- Start healthy ones
- Talk, sing, write, draw, play, sleep, be awake, work, dream, read, color, walk, stretch, relax
- Forgive myself and others
- Build a Good Life

Brain/Mind Connection

You have a brain and you have a mind. They are not the same. Your brain is the physical structure, complex almost beyond understanding. Your mind is harder to define. It is unique to you and it cannot be seen. Only recently has new technology been developed to be able to display brain structures while they are actually functioning.

Brain and mind are not the same, yet they are connected. Like hardware and software, not the same, yet connected. They are interdependent, such that one affects the other. Our brain functions can be affected by many things that happen in or outside our body: viruses, bacteria, allergies, autoimmune or central nervous system disorders, and physical trauma. Our brain disorders can affect our mind functions.

Our mind is affected by many different things as well: traumatic events, habitual ways of thinking, what we focus on. The way our mind functions can affect our brain.

We need a balance of brain and mind health. The tools in this book can help restore a balance between brain and mind. Medication may help, especially to begin change. Consciously changing our mind patterns can be even more effective to make permanent change. Research in neuroplasticity is showing that the brain can be rewired and altered for positive changes in mind and body.

Having a balanced healthy brain and a healthy mind helps us to be able to Build a Good Life.

Challenges

Everybody's got them…. challenges. They could be called difficulties, or hurdles, or hard times. Let's choose language that implies triumph. Let's assume a positive outcome. Don't admit defeat, without chance of winning, before the fight has begun. Do you hear the difference between saying "I am challenged by depression" versus "I'm struggling with depression" or "I am depressed"?

I met a woman while speaking in another state. This was her story:

"For several years I was hospitalized many times a year in psychiatric units in my area. I was stuck in a cycle of depression and anxiety. I didn't know what to do or how to change. One nurse said I was stuck in the system; I needed to break free. I didn't even know what that meant. Then she told me not to identify myself as depressed, to think of

Laurie Kimball

the depression as outside myself, not as myself. Not to announce 'I am depressed.' Instead to say, 'I am dealing with depression.' I think that was the turning point for me. I am not my depression. That is no longer my identity. It has now been five years since I was last hospitalized."

A simple change in the way she identified her challenge was the beginning of a difference in finally changing her life in a positive way.

What can be challenges in life? They can include depression, anxiety, financial setbacks, addiction, grief, unemployment, a new baby, normal teenagers, aging parents, or difficult relationships. You name it! What are your challenges? Whatever they may be, all can be managed, dealt with, and used to improve yourself. All our challenges can become building blocks in the foundation of a Good Life.

Tools

"If your only tool is a hammer, the only thing you see is nails."

If you need to sew on a button, you get a sewing kit. If you cut your finger, you need a first aid kit. When you have challenges, get out *101 Tools to Build a Good Life Manage Life's Challenges.* The same tool won't work for every job. What works on one day may not work on another. Choose the tool you need to get the job done, the job of getting through your day, the lifelong job of Building a Good Life.

Check out the tools in a handyman's toolkit. Some are opposite types: saws and clamps or hammers and crowbars. The tools are different because of the requirements of the job. Acquire new tools and add to your personal toolkit.

Find out what tools others are using. Not all tools are used to build up; some tools are used to wreck, destroy, or pull down. There is a noticeable difference between coping skills and self-defeating behaviors. There is a difference between building a Good Life or destroying one - not only your own life but others - in the process.

The more tools you have available, the better the job of building can be accomplished. As more hours are spent on the job, tools are acquired, usually over time, by learning what is needed, and by observing which tools others are using effectively. It takes time and practice to use a tool. Is it reasonable to expect to master a tool the first time it is used? Or to think that only one tool can be used to complete an entire, complicated job? I don't think so.

My original list of tools came from my own personal life and experiences, from my education and professional experiences. Other people have also shared tools from their lives with me. What's in *your* toolkit? Are you Building a Good Life?

Practice

Mornings came so early! They seemed to come earlier and earlier. It became harder and harder to get up and get going. I had to drag myself up, sometimes with help from my mom. To sleep longer, I began getting my things ready the evening before. I chose my clothes and laid them out, I packed my school bag, making sure I had everything I needed for the next day. I even packed my lunch. It was all so I could get up later and still get to school on time. I didn't know that I was practicing tools to manage one of my first big challenges, which was not correctly diagnosed for 30 years: Seasonal Affective Disorder. This was not even an acknowledged condition when I first began feeling its effects. I was 10 years old, only in elementary school, when those short days and long nights forced me to figure out ways to

Laurie Kimball

make mornings easier for me. Using this concept of managing a challenge turned my thoughts and my life in a different, positive, direction.

Practice takes time, effort, repetition, effort, actual time practicing…. Did I mention effort?   Changing any long-standing habit takes work.

- Practice makes better because nobody's perfect.
- Practice makes permanent so choose what you practice.
- Prepare to practice, know what the desired outcome is in advance.

I chose different tools and practiced so I could Build the Good Life I wanted.

Good?

What good is good? It seems to be an underused and unappreciated word today. When God finished each day of creation He looked at what He created and saw that it was good.

We greet others "Have a good day!", ask a friend "Was it good?" after finding out they attended a movie or play. Do you sigh in satisfaction in the evening and say, "It was a good day!"?

We all have something good in our lives. Yet we may miss the Good Life we have because we are focused on what we don't have yet. Do we overlook the good we have because we think we want something better? Sometimes having all you want doesn't give you everything you need for a Good Life.

Laurie Kimball

The Tools

These tools are written in the first person and in the present tense so you can personalize them, make them your own, and use them right away to help manage your challenges.

Build a Good Life for yourself by managing the challenges you have by using the tools that work for you. Try a tool that might not seem to be useful at first, you might just like it!

They are listed alphabetically, not in any particular order of importance.

The ABC's of Challenges

A challenge is hard and it hurts. I have "been there and done that". It takes hard work and feeling the inner pain to get through my life's challenges. I don't like to be challenged in what I consider a negative way. Yet, just like learning my ABCs in school through repetition, over time I learn to "Always Be Creative" when I am challenged. I slow down, make time for prayer and poetry or walks and talks; things I would be too busy for otherwise. How can I be creatively challenged?

Laurie Kimball

Act "As If"

What stops me from doing the things I want to do? Fear, lack of confidence, feeling foolish? I can act as if I am brave, even if I don't feel that way. If I can act as if I am confident, that feeling will grow. I don't wait for the feelings to come first. I act how I want to be and I discover that the positive feelings I want will follow the positive actions I take.

Acknowledge It

Sometimes I spend so much energy denying how I feel or not wanting to admit what's happening, I don't have anything left to deal with what's really going on inside me. I need to acknowledge my own challenges: I feel depressed, I feel angry, I wish things were different, I am overwhelmed, I am anxious, I am afraid, I am in pain.

It's best for me to name my challenge and acknowledge what I feel. Now I can choose what my next steps could be to manage my challenge and move on with my life.

Laurie Kimball

Alternative Therapies

There are many types of therapies. This is not an exhaustive list of what is available nor is it a prescription. People have been helped by acupuncture, herbs, vitamins, minerals, chiropractic adjustments, hypnosis, aromatherapy, homeopathy, and massage. Also working with naturopaths, nutritionists, allergists, and different types of energy therapists can help manage challenges as well. Is there a trusted alternative I can or would try? I need to be smart, check the credentials of my chosen therapist, and also get references.

Anxiety

Anxiety is a challenge. It does not have to control my life. Anxiety can be managed. What does my anxiety feel like to me? When does it happen? Is it related to my thoughts, or events, or does it seem to come from nowhere?

Imagine: my heart is pounding, stomach is dropping, breathing is faster, hands are shaky and sweaty, I might be light headed. Those may be signs of anxiety - or if I am on a roller coaster, it is excitement and exhilaration! Life is an adventure; ride that anxious feeling. I breathe deeply until the anxiety is manageable or even gone. Or I can imagine anxiety as a wave that rolls to shore, lifts me off my feet for a moment, then is gone.

Laurie Kimball

Ask Questions

I need to take time to ask questions about my challenge:

- What is the bigger picture?
- How could I see this differently?
- What can I do I have never tried before?
- What tool can I use today?
- How would someone I admire manage this?
- Has this ever happened to me before?

I will start a list of questions to ask myself when my challenge arises.

Balance

I fall down if I am not physically in balance. Is there balance in my life? I check my work time versus my time for relaxation. Do I balance my time with children or spouse, friends, relatives or neighbors. Do I balance watching TV and exercising? How is my balance of time alone and time with others?

Are there areas out of balance in my life? What can I add, or subtract, to help me have balance in my Good Life? I can draw a pie chart and assign a slice to each of my activities during an average 24 hours to make sure my life is in balance. What slices do I need to adjust, to add or take out, to maintain a healthy balance?

Bath

"Calgon®, take me away!"; do I remember those commercials? There was someone relaxing in a bubble bath, taking time from a busy life to relax. There are times when warm water, soothing bath oil, refreshing scents, a candle, soft music, and time alone in the tub will take me to a relaxed state. I can try taking a bubble bath for old time's sake. But I do remember to keep my head above water!

Bible

"I am worn out from sobbing. Every night tears drench my bed; my pillow is wet from weeping." (Psalm 6:6) Have I ever felt that way? These words were written over 3,000 years ago. King David was a man who seemed to have everything and still had challenges; he felt overwhelmed at times. Scripture helps me to know I am not alone. It can provide me encouragement and a reminder that God is always with me.

Books

Sometimes I like to read in order to laugh or to cry, sometimes to grow or for encouragement, sometimes for information. There are many useful nonfiction books about depression, stress, grief, anxiety, addiction, parenting, and many other life challenges. I may have favorite fiction books that deal with my challenges or have therapy in the story line that are helpful to read and reread. Sometimes I just curl up to enjoy a good book, to slow down, to take a break. I can also read magazines, newspapers, blogs, emails, or even cereal boxes.

Both/And

Life is more a both/and, rather than just an either/or, situation. I can be grateful *and* want more. I can be anxious *and* confident. I can have two seemingly opposite emotions at the same time! Instead of having to choose only one emotion, only one way of thinking, I can accept both even if I have two. I can be happy *and* sad. I can accept where I am *and* want to change my challenge at the same time.

Laurie Kimball

Calendar

I use my calendar to schedule events, to remind myself of what I need to do today. I also use a calendar to record what happens, to track my moods and my successes, to look for patterns and recurring events.

A calendar can help me understand my ups and downs when I utilize it as more than a way to know the date.

Perhaps I can use different colored highlighters to track family member activities or I can use different colored inks to track my types of appointments. How can I use my calendar more effectively? Does my phone have a calendar I can utilize or would I try an online app?

The Carrot or The Stick

Sometimes a donkey gets a carrot for motivation, sometimes it needs a stick to keep going. There are days when I may need a little something good to get me going. Maybe it's a half hour of a morning news show or a chapter in a good book. Sometimes I do the hardest thing first so I can enjoy a break later. Do I like to vary my daily routine? Or do I find comfort in doing the same activities? As I know myself and manage my challenges, I can choose the appropriate motivational strategy I need for the situation.

Laurie Kimball

Choose A Time

There isn't always enough time in the day for everything. I can choose a time for worry, crying, or anger - whatever my immediate challenge is - and then wait until that time comes to do it. For example: I set my worry time for 8 PM and then during the day if I start to worry, I remind myself that I cannot worry until 8 PM. When the time I set comes, I might not even remember what I was going to worry about. I make time work for me, not against me. I will choose a time to manage my challenge

Clean House

Depression, anxiety, grief, or whatever my challenge is may seem never ending, so it may seem there is nothing I can do about it. I find that chaos in my house intensifies that feeling in me. There can be great satisfaction in beginning a task and finishing it with immediate observable results; polish a mirror and the shine is there right away; vacuum and see results. Just clean it!

Laurie Kimball

Clothes

The saying goes that clothes make the man, or woman, as the case may be. How am I using clothes? As a shield, as a shelter, or as a disguise? What else may influence my choice of clothes? I choose to wear flattering shapes that fit me and colors to enhance my body type. I can dress up to feel more professional or choose casual clothes for play. But I do get dressed every day.

Color

Is life seeming drab and dreary to me? I add some color to my life; paint walls, take a picture of something beautiful and display it. Maybe I will choose a new bedspread or throw pillows. Where can I put color? Sometimes just adding a colored top or blazer, instead of wearing all black, can pick up my mood. I can color or draw a picture with bright colors to brighten my day.

Laurie Kimball

Comic Strips

I love to read the "funny pages". If I have lost my sense of fun I turn to the comics. I clip out and save comic strips that make me laugh out loud. When a situation reminds me of others, I give it to my family or friends. I paste memorable comics in a notebook that I reread when I need a laugh. I can borrow books of favorite cartoonists from the library or visit a bookstore to browse or buy a collection that makes me laugh.

Creative Outlets

I make time for my hobby in my Good Life. I might begin a new interest, learn a new skill, take a class, join an interest group, try something that I haven't done before or haven't taken time to do lately. I like to channel some energy into sculpture, poetry, needlework, martial arts, or something that will show results from my efforts. There are creative physical and mental outlets I can use to vary my activities. I will try something new several times, to first learn to do it and then to evaluate and determine if I enjoy this new experience.

Laurie Kimball

Determination

I am determined to know my challenge, to study it, to learn about it, and to be in charge of it. I determine how I want to live my life, despite or because of my challenge. I don't give up or continue to despair because my life contains challenges. I practice, I learn, I play, I lean on others. I will continue to get up when I fall down, no matter how often I have to!

DIY

Do It Yourself (DIY)! There are books on all types of DIY projects. There are entire stores offering all types of materials and advice to DIYers. There is even an entire television network dedicated to DIY!I can also check out YouTube channels or the many online sources for DIY projects.

Life is a do-it-myself project. I am the only one who lives my life. I need to maintain the structure of my life. Sometimes I have an exciting addition I want to build, sometimes there is only the routine maintenance that is not so exciting. I can read books, take classes about how to maintain, build, decorate, expand my life. When a DIY project goes wrong, there are experts who can help. The same is also true in my Good Life.

Do It Anyway

Feel the fear and do it anyway. Feel the insecurity and do it anyway. Feel foolish and... still do it. Don't let feelings prevent action. I don't know how it will work out until I try. But I won't try an activity if it is illegal, immoral, or unethical. I will go down the sledding hill, try rollerblading, give a presentation or speech, volunteer to teach a class, take a walk, clean a closet. What has been on my list that I choose to do anyway? DO IT!

Do It or View It Differently

If I do what I have always done, I will get what I have always gotten. So, I try a new way to do the same old thing. I view the problem as a challenge and put a positive spin on the challenge that previously I have called a negative situation. I have an opportunity, not an obstacle, in front of me. There is a different view from the roof than from the driveway. I practice other views.

Laurie Kimball

Drama

Drama is focusing on my perception of the intentions of others. It is making situations to be all about me. "Making mountains out of molehills" used to be the expression. If I constantly find myself in drama and chaos, who is the consistent participant in the scenes? Is it usually me?

How much of my life is based on what others are saying about me, or about what others are saying and doing about other people? I make my own choices and decisions. If I want drama in my life, I would rather watch a movie or read a book.

Empty Chair

This is a therapeutic technique that uses two chairs and my imagination to express thoughts and emotions.

I put two chairs facing each other. I sit in one and imagine who I want to speak or express myself to.

What is the challenge? Is it a parent or a relative? A child or a coworker? An emotion, a feeling, or a memory? I talk to the chair and express myself. What do I need to say, yell, cry, explain, demand, remember?

Then I will switch chairs and respond as if I was on the other side of the situation and communicate back.

I consider what I feel, understand, and learn from this.

Laurie Kimball

Examine My Expectations

Is what has actually happened so bad? Or is it that my expectations of the experience have not been met? Are my expectations even realistic? Would anyone be able to accomplish all I have asked of myself or others? Do I expect more from myself or certain others than anyone else? It's good to try some self-examination of my expectations.

Before an experience, I can ask myself what I expect or even hope will happen. Maybe I can lower my expectations or remind myself I am going in with no expectations and will just be in the moment. I live what is happening to me now

Exercise

Do I exercise the recommended 20 to 30 minutes a day, 3 to 4 days a week? When I exercise, my body produces natural endorphins that increase my feeling of well-being. So I will build movement into my day. Start slowly: take the stairs, walk to lunch or to the store or bank, park further away instead of searching for the closest parking spot, maybe go to the gym. I can take someone with me or I can go it alone and enjoy the time and space.

Laurie Kimball

Experiment

In the scientific method, a hypothesis is proposed and experiments are run to test the outcomes. Varying methods are then used to test the hypothesis. Data is gathered and the results are compared. I can try different things to achieve different results in my life. I can collect data while not making judgments to determine if my grand experiment of life is working. If I want to go to bed at night satisfied that I have worked to achieve my goals, then I cannot stay in bed all day. It might be all I want at the moment, yet, at the end of the day it does not make me feel good. I collect data as I observe my life. What experiments do I want to try?

Failure

Where do I get the idea that my life must be perfect or it is worth nothing? Have I forgotten the adage?

If at first you don't succeed,
try, try again.

- How will I learn unless I try?
- If I never try, I can never succeed
- Remember, to fail is the
  First Attempt In Learning
- Try until I succeed
- Fall down and get up again
- It's only failure if I stay down
- It's only failure if I never try
- Think of something I did not do well the first time I tried. How long did I practice until my ability improved?
- Imagine what I would do if I knew I could not fail

Laurie Kimball

Family

Family can be a source of great support, if I let them know what is happening with me. I can relax with people who have known me my whole life. But I am aware that there are "toxic" families which can drag me down as I try to pull myself up. So I examine my family relationships. I find strength in the good memories and in those who have encouraged me. I learn from the bad examples. I find ways not be affected by those "toxic" people who have hurt me. I examine the legacy I am leaving for the family I am a part of now.

Feel It Fully

Is my energy spent on denial? Do I dread my feelings? What do I feel; what do I know? Have my feelings been buried by only being nice or by only being angry? It is important to acknowledge what I feel, to enjoy positive feelings, to express powerful feelings in a safe, non-harmful way. I can write it out, record my words, tell a therapist or a good friend. Sometimes I cry it out or holler. I vent my feelings in non-harmful ways. I will be considerate in how and when I express feelings that involve others.

Laurie Kimball

Foundation

When building, a firm foundation is essential to the entire building. How is my foundation? What is my life built on? Who laid the foundation?

If a foundation is cracked, it can be repaired. It takes work, it takes time, it requires attention. Special tools may be needed. Sometimes the repairs cannot be done alone and an entire crew is necessary to complete the repairs.

If my life is falling apart, I may need to begin by examining my foundation and begin repairs there. I need a supporting foundation for a Good Life.

Four parts of Me

There are four parts of me, just like a four-legged stool. If one leg or an area is missing, I cannot balance.

I have physical, mental, emotional, and spiritual areas. Focusing on one area to the exclusion of the others will result in an unbalanced life. How am I caring for all these parts of me? I can take a walk, work on a puzzle, express a feeling, or say a prayer. What parts am I focusing on and what areas have been neglected? I need to pay attention to all areas.

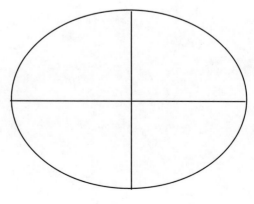

Laurie Kimball

Friends

Friends are there to help me. They can be depended on to give me what I need. It may be a phone call, a lunch out, help with housework or childcare, a walk, an encouraging word, sometimes a challenge, or even a "kick in the pants". I do remember: Don't overuse them, and be sure to be there for them when they need me. I sometimes need "a little help from my friends".

Get Outside Myself

Sometimes I need to find a way to not focus just on myself. How can I do something for someone else? Can I volunteer to help someone? Do I make time to walk the mall and "people watch" - and smile if I catch someone's eye? Could I surprise someone if I send a birthday card, or shovel a driveway, or mow a lawn? I can watch the news or read the paper to catch up with the world. There is more to life than how I feel (I just have to remember to maintain balance!).

Laurie Kimball

Give Myself A Break

Do I expect much more from myself than I would from anyone else? Maybe I need to give myself a break and not get down on myself for a mistake. What would I say to a friend? I need to treat myself as well as I would treat another person. I learn from my mistakes, get on with my life, and don't make the same mistake over and over.

Glass Half...

How do I finish this sentence?
Is the glass half full or half empty?
I can ask that question different ways.

- Should the glass be reengineered to fit the need?
- What if I change the size of the glass?
- If it's half empty can I pour it into a smaller glass?
- Have I ever asked what is in the glass? Do I even want more?
- If I am thirsty, can I just fill it up?
- Am I busy adjusting other glasses?

How else can I look at my challenge? I can practice new ways of defining what is happening. I can turn my challenge upside down, look for another view or look beyond the present circumstances.

Laurie Kimball

Goals

Do I have goals for today, for the year, for my life? Do I have dreams for my life? I have to start somewhere and set some goals for myself. I know it's important to make specific, achievable goals and remember I can never do it better if I never do it the first time. If I never start, I can never finish or even try to reach my goal.

Gratitude

What can I be grateful for, right now, even in my current challenge? When have I ever been grateful? It helps me to keep a list. Sometimes I reach back into the past or sometimes I think about right now. There are hundreds of things I can put on my gratitude list. Even small things count! I can read it over when I can't come up with anything new. I try to add to my gratitude list often.

Laurie Kimball

Grieve

My life doesn't always turn out the way I want it to be. Things happen that are beyond my control. Sometimes I need to grieve for the "might-have-beens" or the "if-onlys". I grieve, but then go on, for I can only live in the here and now. I lose the sweetness of the present if I continue to look for what could have been. If I had never loved, I would never need to grieve the loss of a loved one. I concentrate on the love, not only on my loss. I can seek out a grief group to help me learn and grow.

Have Done List

Sometimes a long "to-do" list can be overwhelming. Instead, I make an ongoing list of all I do during the day and check off items as I finish them. I include anything I may do during the day, such as: take a shower, answer the phone, run an errand, etc. At the end of the day, the list of everything I have accomplished helps offset that "I never get anything done" feeling.

Laurie Kimball

Healing

Healing takes time so I give myself time to heal. Healing is not always the miraculous, instantaneous physical restoration to complete health that most of us want. Healing is also the slow growth of new cells that repair a cut or scrape. I can't always see the change, yet over time, healing happens. I facilitate healing in my life with good nutrition and exercise, with positive thoughts and expressing emotions. I focus on the positive outcome, not ripping off the scab over and over to check for changes. Healing does not always mean a complete cure and it does not mean forgetting how the scar occurred. Sometimes it is an acceptance of what is now. I also think about how I can prevent new injuries.

Humor

3,000 year old advice from the book of Proverbs says "A cheerful heart is good medicine..." Today, it is said that laughter is the *best* medicine. I try to find the humor in my life and laugh every day. I can try watching movies, TV, or I can read books. I can visit a greeting card shop and read the humorous cards. I can share a joke with a friend or ask if they know one. If I look for laughter, I will find it. If I learn to laugh at myself, I will always be amused.

Laurie Kimball

Identify Issues

What are my issues? Have I identified a core challenge, a root cause, gotten way down to the underlying foundation? What may appear to be the challenge may be the result of something deeper. A messy room with clothes strewn about may be the result of not enough storage to put them away neatly. Or am I saving clothes that no longer fit or are not needed for the lifestyle I have now? Is my nonproductive behavior covering up loneliness or anger? What are my continuing issues?

I Don't Know What
I've Got...

Know that song by Joni Mitchell "The Big Yellow Taxi"? She sings "you don't know what you've got 'til it's gone. They paved Paradise and put up a parking lot".

I appreciate what I do have. I realize and appreciate all the positive parts of my life even if everything is not how I would choose it to be. When it's gone, I will treasure the memories and then appreciate what I still have in my life.

Laurie Kimball

If I Have To Go Through It, What Can I Get Out Of It?

I don't waste my suffering. I get gain from my pain. When I face challenges, I think about what I have learned in my life that I did not know before I had that challenge. Do I have more compassion for others, more gratitude for the good days? Do I spend more time on what is important in my life? Do I have opportunity to share what I have learned with others?

What have I already gotten from what I have gone through? What am I getting from what I am going through now?

Ironing Clothes

This is not a tool used often these days, but there are times when it is very satisfying to take a wrinkled garment and, in a few minutes, straighten it out. This is a good reminder that sometimes heat and pressure can smooth something out that would never change if left alone. What pressures in life have been applied to me?

Laurie Kimball

It Could Be Worse...

How could it be worse? Here is a memory from the author: "That was the question I asked when my baby and toddler were sick and my husband was out of town. Then our only toilet overflowed!" What situation like this do I remember? Sometimes I take time to imagine how things could be worse, then I am thankful for what is really happening. There is always someone worse off than me. My situation could always be worse.

It Is What It Is *and*
It's Always Something

Life is what it is *and* something always happens. I can love life, I can enjoy it, I can respond in positive and loving ways. Life is what I make it, after that *something* happens.

I will enjoy the good parts, learn from the hard parts of life, and not be surprised when something happens.
I do go on.

Laurie Kimball

It's a Good Thing That…

What are the good things about my situation? When I am sick or laid up, it can be a good thing to rest, dream, or play games. I find the positives right now, no matter how small, right in the moment. Is the sun shining on my flat tire? Does someone care enough to confront me? It's a good thing that.... I fill in the blank with whatever good I can find despite whatever challenge I am going through at the time.

Journal

A great tool is to start writing how I feel. I can use a beautiful blank book or a spiral notebook. I can date the entries, (it doesn't have to be every day) and write about what is going on in my life, my thoughts, and my heart. No need to write complete sentences or proper paragraphs. I go back and read previous entries when I need to check my progress. What themes or continuing challenges are there? I use the changes I see over time to encourage myself.

Laurie Kimball

Joy List

I can start a list of all the things in my life that bring me joy, even if I don't feel it now. I save it in a notebook or post it where I can see it. What has brought joy to me? I try recalling childhood memories. What has been fun or enjoyable for me? I add to the list as often as I can and I read it over to help bring up joyful memories.

Leaf Blower

When I use a leaf blower, the leaves are gone. But no matter how great a job I do, next fall I will need to get that tool back out again. Sometimes my challenge can return no matter how well I have dealt with it in the past. I am not a bad person or a failure because I am in the midst of my challenge again. I can just get out the "leaf blower" and do the job again!

Laurie Kimball

Lessons

It has been said that experience is a hard teacher; she tests first and teaches later. Education does not end with graduation. There are lessons to be learned every day in life. Some days it feels like I am being tested. In order to remember the lessons I have learned in this school of life, I may need to review lessons from the past. Someone has said that a test is repeated until we pass, until we remember what we have learned. Just like a class, I can take notes to review, to study, and to help me remember what I am learning. What is my lesson in the midst of my challenge? What have I learned? What is something I have gained from my own challenges I would not otherwise know?

Light

Phototherapy, or light therapy, is the treatment of choice for Seasonal Affective Disorder. Other mental and physical conditions may also benefit from application of light. Have I ever noticed what a difference a sunny day makes to me? I add light to my home and office, and let the sun shine in whenever I can. I get outside in natural light every day if possible. I open my drapes, sit by a window, or try to step outside for a few minutes every day.

Laurie Kimball

Listen For Something New

Sometimes I sit wherever I am, close my eyes and just listen. What sounds have I never heard before? I try taking a walk outside and listening. Maybe there is a busy highway near my home that sounds like ocean waves rushing onto shore or maybe it is like wind in the tree tops if I listen carefully. What do I hear outside of my own thoughts?

Live in a what IS world
Not in a what IF world

What world am I living in now? Am I focusing on what I wish life would be if something else had happened? Am I living my life always looking to the past? If all I do is imagine what IF, I will miss what IS. I can look back to learn to make better choices now. I cannot change what happened. I can learn to think about what might happen between different future choices. I won't know for sure what life will be until I accept the choices I did make. I can be prepared for times when I need to ask myself "I might not have planned or chosen this, yet it IS, so what's next?"

Laurie Kimball

Look For Something New

I can sit in a familiar place and just look around. What can I see that I have never noticed before? I try looking around my place at different times of the day. On a walk outside, I try to look for something I have never seen before. What if I safely walk at night and look for differences? I take time to look outside at the life around me and don't always focus on my inner self.

Maintenance

Maintenance isn't usually exciting. It's the year after year, season after season, big and small things that must be done to keep a home in good working order. I do chores like cleaning gutters, weeding around the foundation, and changing the furnace filter. There can be emergency repairs needed if someone throws a baseball through my window.

The same is true in my life. Building a Good Life takes my entire life. Just like a home or garden, there is seasonal maintenance. A virus or accident can lead to emergencies in my life. I take time for maintenance in my life and tend to emergencies as needed. I build and maintain a Good Life.

Laurie Kimball

Manage

The definition of manage is "To be in charge of, deal with, handle".

To be a good manager does not mean that problems do not occur, it means the challenges are handled as they happen. So, I don't despair when my life is not perfect, or dwell on how I wish things were, or put off decisions hoping my challenge will just go away. I live in real time. I manage my challenges, my emotions, and my circumstances.

Mandala

A mandala is a design or pattern. It can be a geometric design that symbolizes the universe. I can draw a large circle on a piece of paper and place a dot in the middle and begin to draw where I am in relationship to my world. I make it nonrepresentational; not exact pictures or specific things. I can use colored pencils, markers, or crayons to color, shape and express my feelings without words. Then I take time to look at the result. What have I expressed?

Laurie Kimball

Massage

There are many benefits to massage: it helps reduce stress, promote healing, eliminate toxins. Best of all it feels good! It's all right to be good to myself, indulge myself, even pamper myself sometimes. For example, I can put lotion on my hands, feet, or my whole body, or maybe exchange massages with a loved one. If I give a back rub to someone, I may get one in return! I can schedule an appointment with a professional. It is good to be kind to my body; it's the only one I have! Where else would I live?

Medical Care

There are physical diseases and conditions that can have emotional changes as a side effect. Central nervous system disorders often have emotional or mental challenges in addition to the physical. Some prescription medication can cause side effects such as depression or anxiety. Such challenges and others can be successfully treated. I may need to get examined by a physician who is also willing to listen to me describe how I feel emotionally as well as physically. Has something changed physically or with new medication that has recently affected my feelings and emotions?

Laurie Kimball

LAUREN,

At an OLLI class I attended last year, the presenter talked about her book:

"101 Tools To Build a Good Life"

It covered so many good suggestions for managing life's many challenges that I decided to purchase the book for myself as well as for all of you grandkids.

I hope you will read it and find some good suggestions in it just as I did when I read it.

WITH MUCH LOVE TO YOU!

GRANDMA LOIS   Christmas

Medication

Medication is not magic although it can be a helpful tool for me. I wouldn't tell a diabetic to skip their insulin because they might get dependent or that they should be able to get along without it. I may need some medication during depression, stress, grief, or other times of challenge. I may work with a health care professional to try out different medications to find what works best for me. It may be a life-long necessity or just a short, limited course to improve my life right now. If I use medication, it needs to be the right medication, at the right dose, taken at the right time. I only use medication as prescribed.

Movies

I love to watch movies. Movies can help me explore issues, make me laugh or cry, encourage me, help me feel relief that things aren't as bad as I thought. There are movies that help me understand the effect of past experiences in my present life. When I watch a favorite movie again, I might hear or see something I have never noticed before. A new challenge in my life may affect what I notice. I live my life; I don't lose it by only watching others' lives on a screen.

Laurie Kimball

Music

Music can affect my emotions. Advertisers know this and use it to their advantage. I can use music purposefully, too. I can crank up the tempo and volume when I need to be energized. I can slow it down when I need to mellow out. I choose music to suit my mood or to change that mood as needed. I can also stir up memories with music or make new ones.

Nap

Thomas Edison and Winston Churchill knew the benefit of taking naps. Just like in kindergarten, when I took a nap for more energy for the rest of my day, I may still need a nap now and then to keep me going. I also remember that a nap implies a short amount of time, NOT sleeping all day!

Laurie Kimball

Nutrition

My body needs proper nutrition to function at its best. What am I feeding mine? Every day I need to eat protein, fruits and vegetables, whole grains, and healthy fats. Do I need to cut down on sugar? I know what I should do, but it is difficult. Could I have unrecognized, undiagnosed food allergies? Maybe I need to have testing or seek advice from experts. It's important to eat right for my body type. If I am what I eat, am I fast, cheap, and easy? Or am I nutritious, healthy, and worth taking time?

On-Ramps

On-ramps are built to help drivers get up to speed as they enter the highway. Most cars need time to accelerate. What will help me ease into my day so I can get up to speed? Maybe I need that first cup of coffee alone, or make my bed and take a shower, or have breakfast with the kids? I may need to build in time to help me accelerate up to the speed of my day.

Laurie Kimball

Photographs

I look at pictures of family and friends to remind me why I go on even when things are hard. Do I have pictures of family times as I grew up? Or of my family today? I can get out pictures of a favorite, relaxing location or of past vacations I have taken. I can look at books or magazines to see sights and places I may never have been to – yet. What do I want to see that will encourage me or help me to relax?

Poetry

I can read poetry to open my emotions or to recognize my feelings. I can write my own poetry; it doesn't have to rhyme. No one else has to read it. I find a place or time to speak my own poetry or read the works of others aloud if that helps. Sometimes when I am challenged, I will write a poem that expresses things I can't say in any other way. I can be a poet, even if I don't know it!

Laurie Kimball

Positive Affirmations

An affirmation is "to endorse, give approval to, support or confirm".

Do I like a good quality in my life or someone else's? It there some way I aspire to be or some positive way I want to think? Have I listened to the way I talk to myself? Is it the same way I would talk to a friend? Am I using positive, not negative, words?

How do I want to be?

How would a friend encourage me? I can encourage myself to practice affirming thoughts.

Some examples:

- I am considerate of others.
- I am an alert, aware driver.
- I am creative.
- I am passionate.
- I like the way I _____(fill in the blank).

Practice

The cliché is Practice makes perfect.

I say practice makes better because nobody's perfect!

A saying of piano teachers is that practice makes permanent, so practice the right way.

I need to know in advance what the desired outcome is in order to prepare to practice properly.

It takes practice to get better at anything. Using tools will help me build a Good Life. I need practice to improve. What am I practicing for in my Good Life?

Laurie Kimball

Prayer

Prayer doesn't magically make a challenge go away for me. But I would not want to be challenged without the resource of prayer to help me. Prayer is available at all times and in all places. Prayer is simply talking to God. No special rituals or preparations are needed. He knows how I feel, and He cares, so I can just be honest.

Prayer Partners

I meet with a friend and we pray out loud together once a week. When challenges get tough, my prayer partner helps me remember our shared history of answered prayer. She even prays for me when I can't pray for myself. I have built-in accountability, so I pray regularly. To have more prayer power in life, nothing beats a partner.

Laurie Kimball

Priorities

Challenges slow me down. I *can't* do everything, so I must slow down and examine my priorities. When I must do less, I do what is most important first. What are my priorities? What is most important in my life? What will I do if I can't do it all? Today I will choose one thing that is a priority to me and spend time on it.

Rename It or Reframe It

Can my problem become a challenge? Instead of being lost, I call it "finding a new way to get there" or "I got here after taking the scenic route". How can I rename my challenge, in a more positive way, that will change how I think about it? The same picture can look very different depending on the matte or frame used for it. I will try rearranging the way I name or frame my challenge.

Laurie Kimball

Resolve Past Issues

Experiences from my past can affect my thoughts and behaviors in the present. Do I repeat behaviors over and over that I didn't want to do again? A past issue may be affecting me now. I can ask friends and relatives to learn more about my childhood to help me understand my past. I can start to journal my thoughts and memories, or try therapy. I don't let the past continue to affect me without making informed choices. When I resolve past issues I don't have to keep reacting for reasons that may have not been clear to me before.

Safe Place

I can prepare a safe place in my mind - and in my life if I need one - to go to when I am overwhelmed, upset, stressed out, or challenged. I set it up and practice going there before I need it in the worst way. I begin by picturing a safe place: Where am I? Inside or outside? Alone or with someone? Day or night? Standing, sitting, laying down? Music or quiet? I breathe and focus. I calm down. I make sure I am physically safe before I go to my safe place in my mind. It's nice to have a cozy, comfortable, actual place as well, but it's not necessary before I can build one in my mind.

Laurie Kimball

Say No

I can become overwhelmed because I have never learned to say "no" to requests from others. I may need to practice saying "no." Maybe I ease myself into a "no" by saying "I'll get back to you" or "I'll let you know" about a request made for my time, energy, commitment, etc. I don't have to say "yes" right away every time someone asks me to do something. I first take the time to think about a request for my time and energy. It might be better to just say "No"!

Schedule

What is my daily schedule like? Will one delay set me back the rest of the day because I am so overscheduled? Do I have to be sick to be forced to take some downtime? Is my schedule realistic? How can I adjust to slow down? I schedule time for myself, for my family, and my friends. I need to remember not to overschedule myself, to build in slack time between appointments. Sometimes, something must give. What can I give up if my schedule is too full?

Laurie Kimball

Self-Anchoring Scale

Draw a line across a piece of paper. Label the left end 0 and the right end 100. First, I rate my satisfaction in life right now on that scale of 1 to 100 and mark it on the line. Next, I rate a happy time of my life and then a difficult time. What is there in common between those times? How can I move my *now* satisfaction rating up the scale?

Right now

1_____100

Happy

1_____100

Difficult

1_____100

Short Sayings

I have a list of sayings that help me get through the day (or through an hour or even just the next minute!):

- I have had tough challenges before.
- I can get through this, too.
- Feelings change. This too will pass.
- Endure the bad. Enjoy the good.
- It's a good thing that___fill in the blank)

What sayings can I add?

What sayings encourage me?

Laurie Kimball

Shower

When challenges drain my energy away or make my life seem dull and uninspired, I can be left with a "why bother" feeling, and it can become easy to let personal grooming go. I will take a shower or clean up every day, even if I don't feel like it. I will make it a habit. Once that invigorating water hits me, I may begin to feel better. Others may appreciate it, too!

Sleep

Do I give myself enough time to sleep? Many Americans are chronically sleep deprived. Most people need 7 to 8 hours of sleep each night. How much time do I give to sleep? There are resources available for me to help design a better sleep routine if needed. I can build my own relaxing routine to help me sleep. What better things do I need to add into my routine? Do I need to eliminate caffeine or alcohol? If I can't sleep, how do I use my time? I could pray, meditate, visualize, remember, plan, or ...

Laurie Kimball

Slow Down

Sometimes I need to allow myself a slower pace when I can just *be* and not *do* for a change. If I live my life at high speed, it may take a flat tire to slow me down. I will take time to live intentionally. I will take time to enjoy the moment I am in, to talk with people around me. I will watch a small child and observe how much "in the now" children live. I will take a day off, or even an hour, to occasionally slow down and smell the roses, literally and figuratively.

STOP Technique

When an unwanted thought or feeling is filling my mind or body—STOP! I stop the challenge by saying *stop* out loud if I can (depending on the situation) or I shout *stop* in my mind to break a train of thought. I have replacement thoughts, statements, songs, or visuals of what I want to think, ready to put in the place of the negative, obsessive, or bad habit. Sometimes it means practicing the STOP technique every hour or even every minute for a while to help manage any obsessive, unwanted thoughts.

Start Thinking Of Positives!

Laurie Kimball

Superpowers: 5 senses

My physical senses are how I experience and explore the world around me. I can ground myself with my senses. I use my sense of seeing, hearing, touching, smelling, and tasting to focus on the here and now. I stop and see, hear, feel, smell, taste, and then describe the experience. My senses help me remain in the present and not be carried off into the despair of the past or experience the anxiety of the unknown. Be here now!

The 4 R's

Old fashioned school taught 3 Rs: Reading, writing, and 'rithmatic.

To build my Good Life I need 4 **R**s:
- Eat Right
- Move Right
- Sleep Right
- Think Right

I need to balance these **R**s in my life.
What good **R** am I choosing now?
What good **R** do I need to add to my Good Life?

Laurie Kimball

3-D Representation

I can build or make something to represent my life, my situation, my recurring thoughts, or whatever it is that's challenging me. I can use my imagination and my hands. I could buy specific materials or use objects from around the house. For instance, I could use different colored beads, with each color representing a different challenge, and string them to represent a timeline of issues in my life. I could draw a diagram of my life. I could list the challenge(s) I have in my life. What can I choose to represent my challenge?

3 Main Questions

There are graduate schools that teach counseling students to ask their clients 3 main questions:

- Where am I now?
- Where do I want to be?
- How will I get there?

So I ask myself these questions.

It can also be helpful to ask:

- How did I get here?

Laurie Kimball

Tears

Scientific research about tears has shown there are different types of tears. This includes tears for the purpose of cleansing emotions. It is okay to just cry if that is what I feel I need to do. If I can't cry on my own, I can watch a movie or read a book that can turn on the tears. However, crying all day, day after day, is a signal that something is wrong. I may need to seek treatment to manage this challenge.

Therapy

Therapy is not a tool that can fix everything in just one day. A helpful and healthy therapeutic relationship can be invaluable for personal growth and resolution of my issues. This takes time. I don't give up if one therapist hasn't helped me, I must be sure the "fit" is right for me. I can interview different professionals and find a therapist that works well with me. It isn't just talking, I must be prepared to do hard, often emotional, work. A therapist can also be used as a consultant on an as-needed basis when I need an expert view to discuss new challenges as they arise as I continue to live my Good Life.

Laurie Kimball

Thought Replacement

A challenge can be an unwanted, unpleasant, or uninvited thought that comes into my mind. I can then replace it with a wanted, pleasant thought. I may examine the unwanted thought, but not dwell on it. I need to have a list, a choice of thoughts I want to think about, to be ready to replace the unwanted ones. So, I spend time to make an actual list. I practice recognizing and replacing thoughts. It may take lots of practice, maybe even by the minute in the beginning, when I become aware and work to replace negative or unhelpful thoughts with positive, encouraging ones. Eventually the intervals will get longer as I focus on chosen replacement thoughts.

To Do List

I can make a helpful list of things to do for the day. I am careful not to list a super-human number of tasks that no one could ever accomplish in 24 hours. I learn to make a reasonable list by practicing and observing what I do actually get done. I mix easy tasks with more difficult ones and include some fun things, too. I do first things first. What I don't get done, I move onto tomorrow's list.

Laurie Kimball

Tool Kit

I imagine my challenge as a home repair project. What is the scope of the challenge? Can I fix it myself or do I need a professional? What tools will I need? Trying different tools out to discover which ones will do the job makes sense. If one tool doesn't work for me today, I don't throw away the entire toolkit, I just try a different tool.

Triple A's:
Aware - Accept - Action

Just like AAA can respond and rescue me to help restore my journey, these three As can help me build my Good Life.

The first **A** is to be **A**ware. Am I aware of my own challenge? Is the challenge that other people annoy me because they complain about an issue that involves me, have some truth to it?

The second **A** is to **A**ccept my challenge. This is my challenge, this is something I want to change.

The third **A** is **A**ction that comes after I am aware and accept my challenge. What can I now do to change?

Laurie Kimball

Volunteer

If I can't get going for myself, sometimes I can get moving for someone else. I can offer my time at a church, school, senior center, shelter, youth club, food shelf, local park, humane society, museum, or other place that needs volunteers. There are many worthwhile organizations that need volunteers to help others. A commitment to others may help bring back a sense of purpose to my own Good Life.

Walk

If I take a walk, I feel better afterwards. I get outside if I can, look for new sights, and listen for new sounds. I can also walk at a mall, on a treadmill, or in the gym. What if I walk with a family member or a friend and discuss my day? If I am alone, I could talk out loud if that helps me. It is good to stretch my legs and myself by walking. I walk every day when and where I can. I could walk while on the phone or when thinking. I could walk to the farthest restroom or drinking fountain. I could park at the far end of the lot. Walk!

Laurie Kimball

Water

My body is mostly water. I need water daily for my health, so I drink 6 to 8 glasses of water a day. Dehydration can manifest itself as hunger, or emptiness, or unsettled feelings. I plan for an easy way to drink more water. I can put lemon, or another fruit or vegetable in my water or get flavored powder or liquid drops to add to plain water. I can make hot or iced tea, buy flavored water, or drink other non-caffeinated beverages. I don't overdo it, because too much water can dilute needed minerals, and that is not better for my body.

What Works for Me?

The best tool is the tool that does the best job. I take time to try out different tools. Doing new work might require new tools. If I do what I have always done, I will get what I have always gotten. I will have the same old results.

Did I find a tool that isn't included in this kit? Add it on the following pages!

Laurie Kimball

Add My Own Tool

Add My Own Tool

Laurie Kimball

Add My Own Tool

Add My Own Tool

Laurie Kimball

Building
Resources

Depression Signs and Symptoms

Can be emotional and/or physical
If you have at least three symptoms that last two weeks or more, please get evaluated.

- Feeling hopeless or helpless
- Inability to concentrate
- Inappropriate guilt or worthlessness
- Recurring thoughts of death or suicide
- Change in appetite or eating habits
- Change in sleeping patterns
- Loss of energy, constant fatigue
- Unusual irritability, anger
- Physical symptoms of unexplained recurring pains
- Lack of interest in activities previously enjoyed

Laurie Kimball

You are not alone

Everyone has faced challenges.

Many people have been depressed, anxious, bipolar, or diagnosed with differing physical and mental health issues and other challenges in life.

You may know some of these:

Abraham Lincoln:
 United States President
Art Buchwald: *humorist, author*
Winston Churchill:
 British Prime Minister
Pat Conroy*: author*
Ernest Hemingway: *author*
Wynonna Judd: *singer*
Marie Osmond: *entertainer*
Sylvia Plath: *poet, author*
Elizabeth Sherrill: *author, editor*
Vincent Van Gogh: *artist*
Robin Williams: *comedian, actor*
Mike Wallace: *journalist*

Tool Tracker

What tools have I tried? How have they worked? When do I use them? Are there certain tools I have never tried? I can use this tracker to watch for my tool use patterns.

Date	Tool	Result

Laurie Kimball

Date	Tool	Result

Date	Tool	Result

Laurie Kimball

Seasonal Affective Disorder Resources

10,000 lux is the recommended intensity for an effective SAD treatment light

Alaska Northern Lights 800/880-6953
www.alaskanorthernlights.com

Aurora Light Solutions 877/670-0342
www.auroralightsolutions.com

Northern Light Technologies 800/263-0066
www.northernlighttechnologies.com

The SunBox Company 800/548-3968
www.sunbox.com

Verilux 800/786-6850
www.verilux.com

The original work on the subject is
*Winter Blues: Seasonal Affective Disorder;
What It Is and How to Overcome It*
Norman E. Rosenthal, M.D.
(Guilford Press,1998)
www.normanrosenthal.com
Also available at Amazon.com
or at your local bookstore

Suicide Awareness - Voices of Education

SAVE is an organization dedicated to educating the public about suicide prevention.

7317 Cahill Road, Suite 207
Minneapolis, MN 55439-0507

Phone: (952) 946-7998
1-888-511-SAVE
Fax: (952) 946 7998
www.save.org
E-mail: save@winternet.com

Laurie Kimball

DID YOU KNOW?
From save.org

Depression can be treated. Of the many millions of Americans who suffer from depression in any given year, the majority can be effectively treated. But only 1 in 3 seek help. It takes time to be accurately diagnosed and to receive appropriate treatment. Take that first step and make an appointment with your health care professional as soon as possible.

Please don't suffer needlessly.

You are not alone. There is help.

The #1 cause of suicide is untreated depression.

IN CASE OF EMERGENCY CALL 911 or 1-800-273-TALK (1-800-273-8255)

**Crisis Text Line
Text: 741-741**

More Resources

NAMI.org

National Alliance on Mental Illness
Excellent education and support
Find online support and locations for state and local meetings

Check your city, county, or state for ACT teams, crisis teams, counseling or drop in centers, support groups, free state text help lines, veterans' crisis lines or other resources. Be selective when checking out online sources.

Don't wait! Connect!

Laurie Kimball

Index of Tools

Laurie Kimball

Laurie Kimball

Thank you for picking up this copy of **101 Tools to Build A Good Life Manage Life's Challenges**.

These tools have worked for me and many others, when they are used regularly. My hope is they will help you build a Good Life. Do you have more tools to add? I would enjoy hearing from you to know what has worked to help you manage your life challenges.

God does make a difference in *my* life. The personal relationship I have makes it possible for me to go on despite the many challenges in life that happen to me and to each one of us. I am not alone in what I go through. You don't have to be alone either. If you would like more information about a relationship with God you can talk to someone at *1-888-NEED-HIM* or go online to www.*NeedHim.org*.

Laurie Kimball

Laurie Kimball

Laurie is available for speaking
and presentations.

For more information contact:

Laurie Kimball RN, M.S.
AGoodLife4U.com

763-360-4127
Minneapolis, MN

Laurie4U@gmail.com

Acknowledgements:

I grew up in a nice town with a nice family and nice friends I still have that gave me a good foundation for life. Even nice isn't perfect.

Mr. Norman Boeve, my high school guidance counselor, now mentor and friend for over 45 years helped me recognize some structural cracks.

Dan Simonson, LP, expert therapist and longtime consultant gave me the leaf blower illustration and helped refine the concept of a personal toolkit.

My prayer partner, Gena, and encouraging friend Beth, both an important part of my life for 30 years, have given me much support.

My husband, Greg, has been the bedrock in our marriage and co builder of three children. Their spouses have been wonderful additions and now grandchildren are a second story.

In 2002 at a community education class I shared my personal list of tools. A participant said "This would make a

great book that I would like to buy!"
The Depression Toolkit: Practical Ways To Get Through The Day was the result.

Thank you to the thousands of people who bought that booklet and shared suggestions, feedback, and tools with me, too many to name.

It needed a remodel and expanded footprint.**101 Tools to Build A Good Life** is the completed result.

Thanks to my first readers for taking time for edits and suggestions: Greg, Dan, Gena, Laura, Mary, Pete, and Scott. I appreciate Lisa Marek as a friend and excellent graphic designer with Art Soul Living. Thanks also to Mic and Gregg at Print Central printers. Any mistakes are my own.

My husband, Greg deserves more than just a third mention. He is my editor, IT guy, tech support, banker, and one heck of a guy, the love of my life!

I hope you all will Build a Good Life, no matter how long it takes!

Order form

101 Tools to Build a Good Life
available by mail for $19.95 each copy.

Mail payment to:
Laurie Kimball
P.O. Box 490584
Minneapolis, MN 55449

Name_____

Address_____

_____

Phone_____

Email_____

Email Laurie4U@gmail.com
for more information